TRAVEL LIKE A LOCAL MILWAUKEE

Milwaukee Wisconsin Travel Guidebook

A.K. Bowen

CZYK Publishing Since 2011.
CZYKPublishing.com
Greater Than a Tourist

Mill Hall, PA
All rights reserved.
ISBN: 9798389304338

>TOURIST

50 TRAVEL TIPS FROM A LOCAL

BOOK DESCRIPTION

Travel Like a Local is a series of travel guidebooks written by local experts to help travelers explore new places like an insider. From learning about the culture and customs to finding the best restaurants and attractions, these guidebooks provide comprehensive information to ensure a hassle-free unforgettable journey. Travel Like a Local in Milwaukee, Wisconsin, USA, by Author A.K. Bowen, offers first-hand and personal insight into the best ways to visit and enjoy "Brew City." Each guidebook is packed with insider tips and recommendations, tailored specifically to the location, so you can make the most of your time and truly get to know the destination. With The Travel Like a Local Guidebooks you'll get the most out of your travels.

OUR STORY

Traveling is a passion of Travel Like a Local book series creator. Lisa studied abroad in college, and for their honeymoon Lisa and her husband toured Europe. During her travels to Malta, an older man tried to give her some advice based on his own experience living on the island since he was a young boy. She was not sure if she should talk to the stranger but was interested in his advice. When traveling to some places she was wary to talk to locals because she was afraid that they weren't being genuine. Through her travels, Lisa learned how much locals had to share with tourists. Lisa created the Travel Like a Local book series to help connect people with locals. A topic that locals are very passionate about sharing.

TABLE OF CONTENTS

DEDICATION

This book is dedicated to my father, who always knew that I would love Milwaukee once I moved here. But I'd also like to give my boyfriend, Logan, a shout-out because he and I get the opportunity to enjoy living in this beautiful city together.

ABOUT THE AUTHOR

A.K. Bowen is a licensed attorney turned fiction writer. She has lived in Milwaukee, Wisconsin, for almost a decade with her boyfriend and their three cats. During the pandemic, she decided to leave the corporate world and pursue her dream of becoming a published writer.

HOW TO USE THIS BOOK

Welcome to the Travel Like a Local Guidebook series! Our mission is to give readers an inside look at travel destinations around the world through the eyes of locals. Each guidebook in this series is written by a local who has explored and experienced the destination in depth. The author has made suggestions based on their own experiences. Please check before traveling to the area in case the suggested places are unavailable.

Travel Advisories: As a first step in planning any trip abroad, check the Travel Advisories for your intended destination.
https://travel.state.gov/content/travel/en/traveladvisories/traveladvisories.html

FROM THE PUBLISHER

Traveling can be one of the most important parts of a person's life. The anticipation and memories that you have are some of the best. As a publisher of the Travel Like a Local, Greater Than a Tourist, East Like a Local, as well as the popular *50 Things to Know* book series, we strive to help you learn about new places, spark your imagination, and inspire you. Wherever you are and whatever you do I wish you safe, fun, and inspiring travel.

Lisa Rusczyk Ed. D.
CZYK Publishing

*"Travel is the only thing you buy
that makes you richer."*

~ Anonymous

Milwaukee
Wisconsin, USA

Milwaukee Wisconsin Climate

	High	Low
January	30	20
February	32	21
March	42	31
April	50	39
May	60	47
June	70	57
July	77	56
August	76	66
September	70	59
October	59	48
November	47	37
December	34	25

GreaterThanaTourist.com

Temperatures are in Fahrenheit degrees.
Source: NOAA

INTRODUCTION

Figure 1 Milwaukee, Wisconsin, is the state's largest city.

Milwaukee is the largest city (population: 569,330 [as of 2021]) in Wisconsin, and it's located in the southeastern part of the state. It's only approximately eighty-two miles away from Chicago, which equates to about an hour-and-a-half drive between the two cities. It's an international seaport and is on the western bank of Lake Michigan.

It's often referred to as "the beer capital of the world" or "Brew City," as it was once home to Pabst, Miller, Schlitz, and Blatz brewing companies (Miller is the only one left).

The city is also called "the City of Festivals," as it hosts more than 100 festivals throughout the year, including the world's largest music festival, Summerfest.

Yet another nickname, "the Cream City," has been bestowed upon Milwaukee because of the dominance of the creamy-yellow bricks used in corporate and residential buildings during the 1900s.

NEIGHBORHOODS

There are 191 distinct neighborhoods, which are generally categorized as Avenues West and Marquette, Brewers Hill, Clark Square, East Town, Historic Third Ward, Riverwest, Westown, Bay View, Bronzeville, East Side, Harbor District, Menomonee River Valley, Walker's Point, and Wauwatosa.

SPORTS TEAMS

Milwaukee has six professional sports teams. Arguably, the teams that pull the most enthusiastic fanbases include the NBA's Milwaukee Bucks (stadium/arena: Fiserv Forum), the MLB's Milwaukee Brewers (stadium/arena: American Family Field [previously Miller Park]), and the AHL's Milwaukee Admirals (stadium/arena: UW-Milwaukee Panther Arena).

Figure 2 The Deer District outside of Fiserv Forum, where the Milwaukee Bucks play.

COLLEGES AND UNIVERSITIES

Milwaukee is home to twenty-five higher-education institutions, including two-year community colleges, technical schools, and four-year public and private universities. There are a number of notable four-year schools, including Marquette University, UW-Milwaukee, Milwaukee School of Engineering, Milwaukee Institute of Art & Design, Medical College of Wisconsin, Mount Mary College, Columbia College of Nursing, Wisconsin Lutheran College, Alverno College, and Cardinal Stritch University.

BENEFITS OF TRAVELING LIKE A LOCAL

There are many benefits of traveling like a local in Milwaukee. For one thing, there's just so much to do, especially in the summer months. So, having complete knowledge of all the festivals and events helps determine the best, most entertaining, and budget-friendly.

HISTORY

Milwaukee (noted in early records to be spelled "Milwaukie") was initially the home of several Native American tribes, many of which spoke the Algonquin language. In fact, as Alice Cooper explained in the 1992 movie *Wayne's World,* the name Milwaukee was derived from the Algonquin word millioke (or as emphasized by Cooper: "mill-e-wah-que"), which is commonly interpreted as "the good land."

People lived in the areas around Milwaukee for 13,000 years before the first white settler arrived.

That man, named Jacques Vieau, was a French-Canadian fur trader who built a trading post overlooking the Milwaukee and Menomonee rivers in 1795. Vieau was a seasonal resident of Milwaukee, and in 1818, Vieau's son-in-law, Solomon Juneau, was given all of his assets in the city. Solomon is considered the first permanent white resident and founder of Milwaukee.

Juneau (along with a man named Morgan Martin) laid out the city's first streets, platted lots, and brought in new settlers. For the next twenty years, Juneau served as Milwaukee's postmaster and mayor, and he built its first store, hotel, and courthouse. He also started the city's first newspaper, *The Sentinel*. (*The Milwaukee Journal Sentinel* is currently the oldest operating business in Wisconsin.)

To this day, Juneau is remembered by local Milwaukeeans. There is a Juneau Avenue downtown, a Juneau Park (in which a replica of his cabin as it was in 1822), a Solomon Juneau High School, and Solomon Juneau, a 22,500-pound bell in the infamous clock tower of Milwaukee City Hall.

Fun fact, Solomon Juneau was cousins with Joseph Juneau, the man who founded the city of Juneau, Alaska.

BASICS

Like the rest of the Midwest, Milwaukee comes with the stereotype of being inhabited by friendly and nice people. And as such, any person planning a meal out should anticipate cheery waitstaff. But also know that they expect to be tipped (at least twenty percent) well based on their courtesy and kind demeanor. The same goes for those who deliver food.

Families traveling to Milwaukee for a concert, festival, sporting event, wedding, etc., are advised to choose accommodations that are as close to the event as possible. This makes travel so that travel can be done on foot and is as seamless as possible.

Milwaukee is a welcoming place for visitors who are part of the LGQTQ+ community. In 2016, it was rated as one of the top ten "Under the Gaydar" cities in the country based on its lively nightlife and hospitality. Milwaukee is also the home of one of the largest and longest-running pride events every year.

Fun fact: This is it! is the oldest operating gay bar throughout the country. It was opened in 1968 by a mother and son duo, June and Joseph Brehm, who both identified as straight, and has since been under the ownership of Trixie Mattel (the drag queen persona of Brian Firkus, a UW-Milwaukee graduate and Wisconsin native, winner of the third season of *RuPaul's Drag Race All Stars*. Local and world-known queens perform there regularly.

BASIC PHRASES FROM LOCALS

One important thing to note is that many Milwaukeeans shorten the city's name to its airport code, "MKE." You will see this version at the end of stores, restaurants, and other businesses throughout the town and its surrounding areas.

Also, anyone who spends enough time in Milwaukee will likely hear of its infamous characters—like "The Milverine," a man named John Hamann who is famous for resembling the famous Marvel character and walking around the city, Brother Ron, a man who drives around in a 1989 Chevy Caprice that is littered with pieces of paper with handwritten Bible verses and controversial quotes, and Dick Bacon, a nudist and fitness-devoted man who could be found by the lakefront at any time of the year.

Aside from famous locals, words commonly uttered in Milwaukee include referring to a drinking fountain as a "bubbler," judging a good cheese curd based on its "squeak" (word to the wise, we take most of our cheese very seriously), and explaining that travel plans include "going up north," referring to the scenic, northern part of the state where many residents have cottages or cabins.

Contrary to popular belief, "bag" isn't the only thing we're known for saying differently than other Americans. Those who have lived in Milwaukee for a long time are often accused of not pronouncing the city's full name. Instead, we tend to leave out the "Mil" and say "Ma-wau-kee." In fact, people throughout Wisconsin are also often found guilty of mispronouncing the name of our own state. A true Wisconsinite can sniff out a local by the way the "con" is enunciated. We sometimes replace the "c" with a "g," so we say, "Wis-gon-sin." A hard "con" can indicate your status as an outsider.

PACKING TIPS

One of the great things about Milwaukee is that it experiences all four seasons, so packing tips will differ depending on the time of year.

In the spring months, the city can be cloudy and rainy. Water-resistant clothing (like rain boots, umbrellas, and ponchos) is useful during that time. In the summer, the weather is often hot and humid. Wearing as little clothing as legally possible (while also potentially carrying along an umbrella if it rains and a sweater if it gets colder at night) is recommended. Conditions in the fall are similar, with the temperature dropping the closer it becomes to winter. So, jeans and long sleeves are advisable during that time. And in the winter, the city doesn't get as much snow as the majority of the state, but it does get cold. So, a coat, scarf, winter boots, and mittens are a must.

But the weather is generally unpredictable, so preparing for a range of temperatures and conditions should be accounted for any trip to Milwaukee. (Seriously, we've gotten snowstorms as late as March or April.)

Besides plenty of clothing options, the only other thing that is an absolute must when planning a trip to Milwaukee is your driver's license. It will be required to get into all of the historic breweries and bars around town. Even if you're sure you look over 21, I'd still bring it, just in case. I'm 31, and I'm still regularly carded. I've even been accused of faking my ID (it wasn't fake at all—I was 23—luckily, I knew one of the other bouncers, so it wasn't a big deal).

GETTING AROUND MILWAUKEE

TRANSPORTATION OPTIONS

On Foot

One of the great things about being in the heart of Milwaukee is the ability to walk almost anywhere you need to go—the pharmacy, favorite restaurants, grocery stores, concert venues, etc.

Rental Cars

Visitors who plan to stay in or travel to the outskirts or surrounding suburbs can always rent a car through companies like Enterprise, Alamo, Thrifty, Hertz, etc.

Uber/Lyft

If you don't feel like driving, Milwaukee has its fair share of ride-hailing apps like Uber and Lyft. These options are especially great for people who plan to drink one too many drinks at a bar, brewery, concert, etc. They keep the passengers and everyone else in the city safe!

Figure 3 Part of a highway in Milwaukee.

<u>Taxis</u>

Although rarer in the era of Uber and Lyft, taxi services are still available in the city, such as Milwaukee Taxi Service, Ltd, Yellow Cab Co-Op Milwaukee, and Discount Taxi Cab MKE. Riders just need to look up particular businesses and call for a driver to arrive and take them to their preferred destination.

The Hop

Since November 2018, residents of Milwaukee have had access to a streetcar service called The Hop. It's sponsored by the Potawatomi Hotel & Casino, and people can ride it for free. You just need to find the right stop for your desired route. The Hop can take you to an event, a restaurant, you name it!

Bike and Scooter Share

For the last couple of years, companies like Bublr Bikes and Bird and Lime scooters have allowed people to basically "rent" equipment through their phones and explore the city. Of course, the bikes need to be returned to designated docks, but the scooters can usually be left anywhere for another potential user to come upon.

Public Bus

For visitors planning to stay in Milwaukee for a more extended period or who may be particularly budget conscious, the Milwaukee County Transportation Services might be the best way to go. You can use an app, get a card, or pay with cash to go all over the city cost-effectively. Then, passengers need to find out what the right stop and route will get them where they need to go. Interactive maps can be found online. Here's a tip: some bus stops are way nicer (have enclosures and are relatively cleaner) than others. So, maybe ask around when trying to discern your best option.

Amtrak Train

For visitors who want to visit other states in the Midwest, the Milwaukee Intermodal Station, located downtown, allows passengers to purchase tickets and board their desired trains. This is an easy and relatively stress-free way for people to travel to Chicago. The train also goes to locations in Indiana, Michigan, and Missouri.

NAVIGATING THE CITY

As stated above, several modes of transportation can be used to navigate this great city. They include rental cars, ride-hailing apps, rental bikes or scooters, The Hop Streetcar, and public transportation.

SAFETY

Milwaukee is a beautiful city, but some parts may be considered safer than others. Of course, this should be considered on a person-by-person basis. Still, everyone should be as cautious as possible when traveling in an unfamiliar city. You can research particular areas of Milwaukee online to determine its general safety. However, speaking with locals once you're here could also be helpful.

ACCOMMODATIONS

HOTELS

It is said that there are over 150 hotels in the Greater Milwaukee Area. So, I have compiled a list based on the "class" of certain hotels to narrow down which suits your needs, preferences, and budgets. I avoided typical chains like Hilton, Hyatt, Marriot, etc. Instead, I focused on hotels that offer experiences that may be unique to Milwaukee.

<u>4 Star</u>

The Pfister Hotel and Spa. An iconic site in downtown Milwaukee and one of the Midwest's premier luxury hotels.

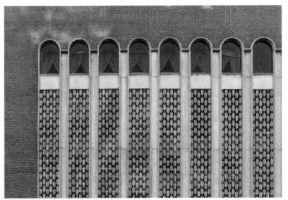

Figure 4 Part of the Pfister Hotel located downtown.

Kimpton Journeyman Hotel. The Journeyman is a top-rated boutique hotel located on the cusp of the Historic Third Ward and downtown.

Hotel Metro, Autograph Collection. This chic boutique hotel, also located downtown, boasts an intimate, art deco style that "redefines luxury and comfort in the heart of the city."

Saint Kate – The Arts Hotel. Deemed by a Conde Nast traveler as "One of the Absolute Coolest Hotels in Wisconsin," Saint Kate is a downtown boutique hotel featuring nationally recognized art in each room.

The Iron Horse Hotel. The Iron Horse is a luxury hotel that celebrates Milwaukee's history through original Cream City Bricks, handcrafted food and drink, an outdoor patio, and more.

The Brewhouse Inn & Suites. Housed in the original Pabst brewery, this hotel is said to have "vintage charm and grandeur" that "sets the perfect stage for travelers coming to Milwaukee."

3-Star

Kinn Guesthouse Downtown Milwaukee. Located near some of Milwaukee's trendiest destinations with curated spaces that combine modern hotel luxury and the comforts of your home. There is also a location in another neighborhood called Bay View.

The Knickerbocker on the Lake. A historic Milwaukee hotel located right on Lake Michigan's shores. It features the Knick Restaurant and Knick Salon & Spa.

Hostels

A building called Cream City Hostel opened in 2019 and was designed to be "a budget-friendly alternative with clean and cozy accommodations that make [it] a great place to get a good night's rest." Unfortunately, the owners announced on their website shortly after that it would be closed and instead converted into a housing cooperative.

<u>Airbnb</u>

There are plenty of Airbnb options to choose from in the city. Visitors can narrow their options based on the main attraction that will be visited, whether it's the Harley-Davidson Museum, the Milwaukee Art Museum, American Family Field, the Milwaukee County Zoo, etc.

SIGHTSEEING

BEFORE YOU LEAVE

Any fan of Happy Days, the classic TV sitcom would be remiss to make a visit in Milwaukee and *not* take a picture with "The Bronze Fonz," which is located along the River Walk.

In terms of more or less prominent locations, I mention a lot of other "must-sees" throughout the rest of this guide and in the top 50 reasons to visit Milwaukee.

HOW TO DRESS

In general, Milwaukeeans are casual people. Unless you're going to an overly fancy event that states otherwise, the "no shirt, no shoes, no service" rule typically applies.

PICTURES TO TAKE

Figure 5 Part of the Milwaukee River.

Aside from the already mentioned "Bronze Fonz," must-have pictures in Milwaukee include the Villa Terrace Decorative Arts Museum, which gives you a beautiful backdrop of Lake Michigan, Finks bar that has a long "Hello Milwaukee" mural on the side of the building, The Pink House, Atwater Beach, Black Cat Alley, which is full of fun and pretty murals, and the Milwaukee River Walk. I would also recommend getting a photo near "The Calling," a large, bright orange "sunburst" sculpture outside the Milwaukee Art Museum. Although I must tell you, some locals call it "Milwaukee's butthole."

Maybe consider including that in the caption of your photo? #MilwaukeeButthole, anyone?

Figure 6 Part of "The Calling," which was added to Milwaukee's horizon in 1982.

TOURIST ATTRACTIONS

MILWAUKEE ART MUSEUM

Figure 7 The Milwaukee Art Museum sits right on the beautiful Lake Michigan.

The art museum, part of which served as the setting for the home of Patrick Dempsey's character in *Transformers: Dark of the Moon*, is located overlooking the beautiful Lake Michigan and has traveling shows come through and a more permanent collection of over 32,000 pieces, including paintings, decorative arts, photography, installation art, drawings, sculptures, and more. Of note is a large Georgia O'Keeffe, a Wisconsin native, collection housed at the museum.

Figure 8 Inside of the Milwaukee Art Museum.

You can see all of it for only $22 per adult (prices are reduced for military, senior citizens, and children).

The collection can be seen online based on category (artist's nationality, object type, themes, etc.) by visiting collection.mam.org.

Figure 9 The Quadracci Pavilion of the Milwaukee Art Museum.

This museum is the only one of its kind to have "wings" that open and close based on the building's hours of operation. The mechanism, known as the Burke Brise Soleil, is a moveable sunscreen that rests atop the part of the museum known as the Quadracci Pavilion, designed by Spanish-born architect Santiago Calatrava.

Other buildings and sights are considered part of the museum, including the War Memorial Center and the Cudahy Gardens.

Figure 10 The War Memorial and Art Center.

HARLEY DAVIDSON MUSEUM

Figure 11 The emblem on a Harley Davidson motorcycle.

This museum is perfect for anyone interested in celebrating
Harley's history (spanning over 100 years)! And the museum is perfectly at home in Milwaukee because it has been headquartered here since its inception in the early 1900s! There are 450 motorcycles to see, including the exact replica of the bikes Peter Fonda and Dennis Hopper rode in *Easy Rider*, including Fonda's "Capitan American" and Hopper's "Billy Bike." Plus, the semi-permanent collection includes the actual 1956 KH owned by Elvis Presley. This upcoming summer is the perfect time to plan a trip to the museum because it is the 120th anniversary of Harley Davidson, and there will be a four-day festival to celebrate the occasion between July 13-16.

BREWERIES

We are the city that beer built, and no visit to Milwaukee is complete without a trip to one of its many breweries.

Best Place and the Historic Pabst Brewery

Figure 12 A can of the famous Pabst Blue Ribbon Beer.

917 W. Juneau Avenue
Milwaukee, WI 53233

Phone: (414) 630-1609
info@mkeimages.com
bestplacemilwaukee.com

Hours of Operation
Sunday through Friday – 11:30 a.m. to 5:30 p.m.
Saturday – 10:30 a.m. to 5:30 p.m.

Daily tours about the history of Midwestern beer are available in this historic building, which once served as Pabst's corporate headquarters and is located in the downtown area.

Guests will learn about and sample beer while marveling at the intricate German architecture and enjoying two beautiful outdoor courtyards.

Black Husky Brewing

909 E. Locust Street
Milwaukee, WI 53212

Phone: (414) 763-4141
toni@blackhuskybrewing.com
blackhuskybrewing.com

Hours of operation:
Sunday – 12 to 7 p.m.
Monday-Friday – 4 to 9 p.m.
Saturday – 12 to 9 p.m.

This award-winning brewery is perfect for lovers of beer and huskies! It is located in the Riverwest neighborhood of the city, and it was first founded to honor the 23 dogs in the owner's sled dog kennel. While sampling Black Husky beers, you may also get to listen to live music, play trivia, or participate in the other events the brewery puts on.

Other fun information:
- It was Wisconsin's first Nano-brewery, which opened in 2010.
- The massive log bar was made by the owner and transported to Milwaukee in 2016.
- It was the first recipient of the Joe Bartolotta Award for contributions to the community.

City Lights Brewing Company

2200 W. Mt. Vernon Avenue
Milwaukee, WI 53233

Phone: (414) 436-1011
nikki@citylightsbrewing.com
citylightsbrewing.com

Hours of operation:
Monday-Thursday – 3 to 9 p.m.
Friday-Saturday – 11 a.m. to 10 p.m.
Sunday – 11 a.m. to 8 p.m.

This brewery is located in the 115-year-old Milwaukee Gas Light Building. And it mixes modern-day brewing and historic architecture. Tours of the brewery itself are available on Fridays and Saturdays.

Other highlights include the fact that their Hazy IPA earned a Silver Medal at the Great American Beer Festival for Juicy/Hazy IPA, their Mexican Lager and Coconut Porter both won a Gold Medal in the World Beer Championship, and it was named 'Patio with the Best Hanging Flower Baskets in Milwaukee' with a 10' basket circumference.

Explorium Brewpub

5300 S. 76th Street, Suite 1450A
Greendale, WI 53219

Phone: (414) 423-1365
exploriumbrew.com

Hours of operation:
Sunday – 11 a.m. to 9 p.m.
Monday-Thursday – 11 a.m. to 10 p.m.
Saturday – 11 a.m. to 12 a.m.

This unique brewery is located in Southridge Mall. Tours (by appointment only) on Fridays and Saturdays explore the process and particular challenges of brewing beer in a mall.

Gathering Place Brewing Company

811 E. Vienna Avenue
Milwaukee, WI 53212

Phone: (414) 635-0569
joe@gatheringplacebrewing.com
gatheringplacebrewing.com

Hours of operation:
Monday-Friday – 4 to 10 p.m.
Saturday – 2 to 10 p.m.
Sunday – 2 to 6 p.m.

This is another Riverwest brewery, and it offers tours to get a look behind the scenes on Saturday at 3 p.m. and Sunday at 2 p.m.

Other highlights include a wide range of brewing styles from German lagers to double IPAs to Nordic farmhouse ales; it donates at least 1% of sales to local non-profit organizations; and has an industrial-chic taproom with I-beam cathedral entrance.

Good City Brewing- Westown

333 W. Juneau Avenue
Milwaukee, WI 53203

Phone: (414) 539-4343
info@goodcitybrewing.com
goodcitybrewing.com

Hours of operation:
Monday – Closed
Tuesday-Saturday – 11 a.m. to 12 a.m.
Sunday – 11 a.m. to 10 p.m.

The most recent location of Good City Brewing is located in the heart of the Bucks' Entertainment District, and it includes a taproom, restaurant, and 350-seat private event space. It houses the company's pilot brewing system and wild ale program.

Miller Brewery

4251 W. State Street
Milwaukee, WI 53208

Phone: (414) 931-BEER
millerbrewerytour@millercoors.com
millerbrewerytour.com

This tour offers a journey through more than 160 years of brewing history—from Fredrick Miller's arrival to Milwaukee to the high-speed production lines used today. You can also peek into the famous hand-dug Miller Caves, which Frederick Miller used to chill his beer. Tours are on Thursdays and Fridays and are on a first-come-first-served basis.

The Bavarian Bierhaus

700 W. Lexington Boulevard
Glendale, WI 53217

Phone: (414) 236-7000
info@bavbierhaus.com
thebavairanbierhaus.com
Hours of Operation- 11 a.m. to 10 p.m.

Visitors will experience Milwaukee's German hospitality while enjoying a restaurant, beer garden, and brewery. Free tours are available every Friday from 4:30-6:30 p.m. and run every half hour.

Their Biers are made fresh in the brewery, and this Bierhaus hosts the largest, oldest, and most authentic Oktoberfest in the Midwest.

Lakefront Brewery

1872 N. Commerce Street
Milwaukee, WI 53212

Phone: (414) 372-8800
info@lakefrontbrewery.com
lakefrontbrewery.com

Hours of operation:
Monday-Thursday – 4 to 9 p.m.
Friday-Saturday – 11 a.m. to 9 p.m.
Sunday – 1 to 5 p.m.

This brewery tour was ranked on TripAdvisor as one of the nation's top four best brewery tours. Daily tours through Lakefront are known for being full of jokes and beer breaks.

On a particularly amusing note, the tour typically includes putting a glove on the bottles and singing the theme song from *Laverne and Shirley*.

Fun fact: Lakefront Brewery created the first ever USDA-certified gluten-free beer.

Figure 13 An art installation outside of Lakeside Brewery.

Mobcraft Beer

505 S. 5th Street
Milwaukee, WI 53204

Phone: (414) 488-2019
events@mobcraftbeer.com
www.mobcraftbeer.com

Hours of operation:
Monday-Thursday – 3 to 10 p.m.
Friday-Saturday – 12 p.m. to 11 p.m.
Sunday – 12 p.m. to 10 p.m.

Although this brewery was founded in Madison, Wisconsin's second-largest city, it was transplanted to Milwaukee and is located in Walker's Point. Tours are offered on Saturdays.

You'll also find a low pHunk Sour Ale, which won a gold medal at GABF 2019, a gold medal at World Beer Cup 2022, and a bronze medal at GABF 2022, 31 tap lines, and education about the extensive Wild & Sour Program.

Third Space Brewing

1505 W. St. Paul Avenue
Milwaukee, WI 53233

Phone: (414) 909-BEER
info@thirdspacebrewing.com
thirdspacebrewing.com

Hours of operation:
Monday-Thursday – 4 to 9 p.m.
Friday – 2 to 10 p.m.
Saturday – Noon to 10 p.m.
Sunday – Noon to 7 p.m.

This space transformed a historic Menomonee Valley factory and turned it into a production brewery and family-friendly taproom and event space. Brewery tours and a large outdoor garden are available.

Other interesting highlights include the fact that it was named one of the 34 hottest breweries in America by Thrillist in 2021, it was named one of the 50 fastest-growing breweries in the U.S. by the BA in 2018, it is the winner of four Great American Beer Festival Medals in four years, and it is the home to Happy Place Midwest Pale Ale.

Sprecher Brewery

701 W. Glendale Avenue
Milwaukee, WI 53209
Phone: (414) 964-2739
beer@sprecherbrewery.com
sprecherbrewery.com

Hours of operation:
Monday-Saturday – 11 a.m. to 9 p.m.
Sunday – 11 a.m. to 4 p.m.

This is one of the best tours available for families because the adults can sample European-style beers (and kids can try famous gourmet sodas) while learning about the brewing process of both alcoholic and non-alcoholic beverages. Tours are available Wednesday through Sunday.

Other fun facts include that Sprecher craft soda and beers are fire-brewed using direct-flamed brew kettles, and Sprecher is one of the last breweries in the U.S. to still do this. Further, Vice President Kecia Sprecher has been part of the company since its inception—her father, Randy, made the famous root beer for her growing up on their family stove. And Sprecher uses local Wisconsin honey in most of the soda products.

Urban Harvest Brewing Company

1024 S. 5th Street
Milwaukee, WI 53204

Phone: (414) 249-4074
steve@urbanharvestbrewing.com
urbanharvestbrewing.com

Hours of operation:
Thursday-Friday – 4 to 9 p.m.
Saturday – 1 to 8 p.m.

Established in 2016, this brewery brews fresh, handcrafted ales in small batches several times a week. There are 11 year-round beers and five seasonal/rotating beers on tap. It also has a spacious and bright Taproom.

A fun fact is that Urban Harvest Brewing Company is located in Milwaukee's most historic and diverse neighborhood, Walker's Point.

Delafield Brewhaus

3832 Hillside Drive
Delafield, WI 53018

Phone: (262) 646-7821
delafieldbrewhaus.com

A tour of this brewery will leave you with two great souvenirs: a photo op on the brewing platform and a logo pint glass you can keep. Tours are available on Saturdays by appointment.

City Tours MKE

1130 N. 9th Street
Milwaukee, WI 53233

Phone: (414) 209-4808
info@citytoursmke.com
citytoursmke.com

If you can't decide which breweries you want to tour, you can count on City Tours MKE to make the decisions for you! For just $80, you and your 21+ family and friends can visit Milwaukee's Brewery District, Third Ward, Fifth Ward, and Bayview. Have you ever tried Snake Oil Nitro Stout, a Harry Cherry, or a Spare Time? These are just a few of the delicious drinks you will encounter on a brewery tour around Milwaukee.

LOCAL HOTSPOTS

<u>Parks and Gardens</u>
There are over 150 parks (covering 15,000 acres) of parks in Milwaukee County. Of those, here are the top 21:

1. Atwater Park—Capitol and Lake Drive, Shorewood

Figure 14 The nautical-themed Atwater Park.

Atwater Park is nautical-themed and was installed in 2015. It offers a spectacular view of Lake Michigan. When the kids are done playing, your family can stroll down to Atwater Beach and let them splash around in the water.

2. Back Bay Park—2315 E. Back Bay, Milwaukee

This park and unique playground are perched along Milwaukee's lakefront. It's also close to local favorites like Colectivo on the Lake, Beans and Barley, Whole Foods, and the East Side Public Library.

3. Carver Park—911 W. Brown, Milwaukee

This huge play system is centrally located just minutes from downtown, and it has a splash pad. So, if you're visiting Milwaukee in the summer months and want to tucker your children out, this park is perfect for you and your family!

4. Estabrook Park—4400 N. Estabrook Dr, Shorewood

Estabrook Park is located on the bank of the Milwaukee River. It has a dog park and a great beer garden next to the playground, so you can enjoy a pint and a giant pretzel while your kids play.

5. Fox River Park—W264 S4500 River Road, Waukesha

This park has slides built right into the hillside, a climbing web, boulders, a sandbox, and more. There are also paved trails that are great for biking or hiking.

6. Grant Park—100 E. Hawthorne Ave, South Milwaukee

   There are four playgrounds in this park. And you can hike the Seven Bridges trail or visit the beach nearby. It also offers picturesque views of Wisconsin's nature.

7. Hart Park—7300 W. Chestnut, Wauwatosa

   Designed as a tribute to the Menomonee River, indigenous people, and the Schoonmaker River, this park is filled with fun and one-of-a-kind equipment. There are also great trails nearby.

8. Hartung Park—Corner of W. Keefe Avenue and Menomonee River Parkway

   Located on the old Hartung Quarry site, this park has a playground, a spider-man-like web, and sculptures of creatures that resemble those that would have lived there when it was still underwater.

9. Hawthorn Glen—1130 N. 60th Street, Milwaukee

   This nature center allows exploration into the woods, a restored prairie, and the Little Nature Museum.

10. Kayla's Playground at Franklin Woods Nature Park—3723 W. Puetz Road

    Built to honor the memory of Kayla ("KK") Runte, a local young girl diagnosed with cerebral palsy who unfortunately lost her life at the age of eight, this park is a beautiful and peaceful playground for kids of all ages.

11. Marcus DeBack Playground—5500 W. Wright Street, Milwaukee

    This park was also named in honor of a young Milwaukeean named Marcus DeBack, who was gone too soon. It features a zip line, lots of climbing equipment, a walking track, fitness equipment, basketball courts, and a 10-foot-tall rope dome.

12. Northwestern Mutual Community Playground @ Summerfest—Henry Maier Festival Park, Milwaukee

This entertainment space offers families inclusive and accessible play for children between the ages of two to 12. Amenities include:

- Enhanced play equipment.
- A toddler play area.
- A flexible programming space (a stage structure and a viewing area for over 500 people).
- Family restrooms.
- Nursing mothers stations.
- Sensory rooms.

13. Playground at Malone—3953 S. Casper Drive, New Berlin

The people of New Berlin helped design and build this park, and there's a little free library there too.

14. Possibility Playground—498 N. Lake Street, Port Washington

Visitors can expect a pirate ship, a rain wheel, and a motion platform at this park. There are also slides, bridges, monkey bars, tunnels, a lighthouse, a rock wall, a chain walk, and balance beams. In addition, a "Tot Lot" includes a fairytale castle, bouncy bridge, police car, and a raised sandbox. And the music area features palm drums, metallophones, and an alligator-shaped drum.

15. South Shore Park—2900 S. Shore Drive, Milwaukee

On Saturdays in the warmer months, this park is perfect for families because it is close to one of the best farmer's markets in the city. But any other day of the week, the park is still great because it overlooks the water, includes exercise equipment for adults, and is near the beach and a beer garden.

Washington Park—1859 N. 40th Street, Milwaukee

This park, which used to be the home of the Milwaukee County Zoo, has over 100+ acres and includes a series of pocket parks with climbing structures—all done in a natural theme. At the end of the park, there is a large playground with an old-fashioned merry-go-round near it. Plus, it is also home to one of the Urban Ecology Centers.

16. Lake Vista Park—4001 E. Lakeside Avenue, Oak Creek

Formerly an industrial site, this park was turned into a gorgeous park along the lakeshore. It features a colorful and engaging playground, a pavilion for special events, and a large open field.

17. Southgate Playfield—3300 S. 25th Street, Milwaukee

This park was revamped in 2020 and has new playground equipment, a splash play area, natural turf playfield, shade trees, a walking loop, and a basketball court.

18. Willowbrooke Community Playground—N97 W6375 Lexington Street, Cedarburg

   This community and volunteer-driven project was created to foster learning, growth, and imaginative play for children of all abilities. It was finished in the early summer of 2019, and it features a merry-go-round, safe surfaces, numerous swings, and more.

19. Veterans Park—located near Lake Michigan towards the downtown area.

   This park doesn't have a playground, but it is still family friendly. You can rent paddleboats shaped like swans across a small lake or have a cookout. And when you reach   the   southern end of the park, you'll find the reason for the park's   name—the Southeastern Wisconsin Vietnam Veterans Memorial. It is made up of three red granite columns that   represent the soldiers in the Vietnam War who were killed in   action, missing in action, and returned home. There are also 11   smaller surrounding columns that represent each year of the   war.

20. Lake Park—2975 N. Lake Park Road.

Like Vietnam Park, Lake Park does not have a jungle gym, but it is considered an urban park with a mix of trees, wide open spaces, walking trails, and a small waterfall. There are also tennis courts, a soccer field, a golf course, and picnic areas. And if you follow the Oak Leaf Trail, you will eventually come upon the North Point Lighthouse. You can even ascend the tower, but it takes 84 steps and a ladder to reach the lantern room.

BOOKSHOPS

There is a solid local bookstore scene in Milwaukee, and here are just a few examples that can be found around town.

Boswell Book Company

2559 N. Downer Avenue
Milwaukee, WI 53211
(Located in the Downer Lakeview Commons)

Phone: (414) 332-1181
Boswellbooks.com

Hours of operation
Sunday – Saturday: 10 a.m. to 8 p.m.

Opened in 2007, the Boswell Book Company has been a staple of the Milwaukee literature scene ever since. Owner Daniel Goldin wanted to create a local bookstore that could survive the digital age and bookstore giants. He also makes sure to employ incredibly knowledgeable booksellers, and they can guide you to the perfect book suitable to your desired genre. There are also frequent events where visiting authors read from their most recent books and answer questions from the audience.

Downtown Books Bought & Sold

624 N. Broadway Street
Milwaukee, WI 53212

Phone: (414) 224-1799
Downtownbooksonline.com

Hours of operation
Sunday: 10 a.m. to 7 p.m.
Monday – Saturday: 10 a.m. to 5 p.m.

This used bookstore has stacks of books for you to peruse. Or, if you have books to sell, you can cash in with books you've previously loved combing through.

Renaissance Books

5300 S. Howell Avenue
Milwaukee, WI 53207

Phone: (414) 747-4526
Renaissancebooksto.wixsite.com

Hours of operation
Sunday – Saturday: 8:30 a.m. to 6:30 p.m.

**Figure 15 A plane outside of the General Mitchell
International Airport.**

You might not always think, "Hey! Let's check the
airport for the next best read." But that is the case for
this bookstore. It is located inside of the main
terminal of the General Mitchell International
Airport. In this store, there are a wide variety of
books that are new and used.

But Renaissance Books wasn't always located in the
airport. It used to be housed in a building at 834 N.
Plankinton Avenue (downtown Milwaukee).
However, it had to close in 2011 because there were
too many books, and shelves and floors were sagging.

<u>Voyageur Book Shop</u>

2212 S. Kinnickinnic Avenue
Milwaukee, WI 53207

Phone: (414) 210-3309
Voyageurbookshop.com

Hours of operation
Sunday – Monday: Noon to 5 p.m.
Tuesday – Saturday: 10 a.m. to 8 p.m.

This is the perfect place to find relatively rare books—including first editions and signed copies (the stuff of book lovers' dreams!).

The Milwaukee Public Library

Figure 16 Outside of the Milwaukee Public Library, the largest public library in Wisconsin.

814 W. Wisconsin Avenue
Milwaukee, WI 53209

This library was established in 1878. It has a main central library and 13 branches, all of which are part of the Milwaukee County Federated Library System. Further, it is the largest public library system in Wisconsin, and there are books to buy or loan. Plus, there's a really cool rooftop garden to read in.

EATING AND DRINKING

Traditional Cuisine and Restaurants

Contemporary culture and traditions brought by immigrants—including Polish, German, and Italian—are to thank for the meals and dishes enjoyed by Milwaukee's residents.

Speed Queen Bar-B-Q

In the summer of 1956, Betty Gillespie and Leonard took their family barbeque recipe and secret sauce and started selling meat out of the back of a storefront. Soon, word grew, and Gillespie was dubbed the "Speed Queen."

Speed Queen Bar-B-Q is now said to use the largest BBQ pit in all of Milwaukee and produces "the finest barbecued meats" with their "trademarked secret sauces," according to their website. It's important to note that this restaurant accepts cash only (and has an ATM on-site).

Fish Fry

Developed by Catholic immigrants whose religion dictated that only cold-blooded animals, like fish, could be eaten on fasting days, such as lent and further populated during the Prohibition era when pubs and taverns needed to think of alternative ways to make money, the Friday Fish Fry is a staple among all of Wisconsin, of course, Milwaukee included. The beer-battered fish (usually cod, haddock, or perch) is traditionally accompanied by lemon slices, cole slaw, tartar sauce, a slice of rye bread, and a potato of some kind.

Cheese Curds

As mentioned earlier, the stereotypes are true, Wisconsinites love all things cheese—especially when in the form of a curd. Whether fried or not, the by-product of baby cheddar that has not had the chance to age over twelve hours is delicious as a side dish or snack.

Frozen Custard

Also alluded to before, Milwaukee is known by many other nicknames. "The unofficial frozen custard capital of the world" because it has the most frozen-custard shops in the world. Although the treat was actually invented in New York City, it was brought to the Midwest during the 1933 World Fair in Chicago. What makes this dessert different from regular ice cream is the addition of egg yokes to make it thicker.

Cannibal Sandwiches

Although it's ill-advised by most health professionals to consume this dish, it is still popular throughout areas of Wisconsin to this day. It involves the use of raw beef and onions, seasoned with salt and pepper, between two slices of rye bread. It is believed that German immigrants inspired these sandwiches because they have a similar dish called "mett" or "hackepeter" that requires similar ingredients.

Real Chili

Figure 17 Real Chili continues to be a go-to for Milwaukeeans today.

First opened in 1931, Real Chili has been a go-to stop for Milwaukeeans for over ninety years. The restaurant, located all over the city, mainly features customizable chili, spaghetti & bean bowls, and hot dogs. Other items, like spaghetti & beans, subs, nachos, and tacos, are also offered (options vary depending on the location).

Hot Ham and Rolls

Although the origins of this dish are unknown to many non-natives and even disputed amongst seasoned Milwaukeeans, one thing is for sure, it has been a long-standing tradition in the city to eat hot ham and rolls on Sunday mornings.

Cream Puffs

Every year during the Wisconsin State Fair, over 400,000 cream puffs are consumed in less than two weeks. They are buttery, flaky pastries that are filled with fresh cream.

Ma Baensch's Marinated Herring

With the slogan of being a "Kiss of Health Since 1932," Ma Baensch's Marinated Herring has been a staple on families' dinner tables in Milwaukee and throughout the Midwest for decades. Lina "Ma" Baensch and her family made and sold pickled herring for seventy years in Milwaukee before the business was sold in 1999, and new ownership took charge. Baensch was said to use only the highest quality herring filets imported from Norway and marinated them in her secret wine or cream sauces beforehand, packing them into jars to be distributed to grocery stores. As of 2021, the products have been made by a co-packing company in Minnesota.

Bratwursts

With a thicker and heavier texture than a regular hot dog, brats were first brought to Milwaukee by German immigrants. At least in Milwaukee, brats are typically prepared with hot mustard, sauerkraut, and sweet relish or another amalgamation (typically including ketchup) of condiments. Brats are eaten throughout the year, but most commonly during the summer at cookouts.

Saz's

What started as a state house (designed to be a first-rate restaurant and sports bar) in 1976, Steve Sazama's company has since branched out into an entire hospitality group that offers catering. Saz's is known for featuring fan favorites like its signature BBQ baby back ribs and BBQ pork sandwich.

Butter Burgers

Since 1885, the butter burger has been a pinnacle of traditional Wisconsin dishes. As the name suggests, everything in the burger is cooked in butter—the meat patty, the onions, and the bun. All of it. After that, a slice of cheese is added on top to complete the sandwich.

<u>Milwaukee-style Pizza</u>

Italian immigrants are responsible for developing the Milwaukee-style pizza, which has a really thin crust, is cut into squares, not triangles, is often cooked in a wood-fired oven, and is traditionally topped with sausage, mushrooms, and onions.

Traditional Alcoholic Beverages

<u>Old Fashioned (Sweet)</u>

The star of this drink is brandy, which is consumed in Wisconsin more than in any other state, and it also involves sugar cubes, bitters, lemon-lime soda, an orange wedge, and a cherry.

<u>Old Fashioned (Sour)</u>

This involves all of the same ingredients as above, but instead of the soda, sour mix or grapefruit soda can be used. The fruity garnishes are substituted with olives, Brussels sprouts, or mushrooms.

Bloody Mary

Figure 18 The bloody mary is a beloved alcoholic beverage and often enjoyed with brunch.

This brunch staple combines tomato juice, clamato, vodka, garlic powder, garlic salt, red pepper, Worcestershire sauce, horseradish, and A1 steak sauce. But the garnishes are where this drink truly shines, and they typically include cheese, pickles, celery, and some kind of meat stick or shrimp. Lemons, green olives, and mushrooms are also sometimes used. And in some places, entire fried chickens are put on the top.

Of course, any Bloody Mary in Wisconsin is accompanied by a beer chaser. Of course, any Bloody Mary in Wisconsin is accompanied with a beer chaser.

Tom and Jerry

Although this drink originated in New England, it made its way to Wisconsin in the 1800s, and it's been popular here ever since. It is a combination of brandy (I told you that Wisconsinites love this stuff), dark rum, hot water, eggs, salt, vanilla extract, butter, powdered sugar, nutmeg, cloves, and allspice.

POPULAR BARS

Figure 19 The Up-Down is a videogame-themed bar on the East Side of Milwaukee.

This is tough because Milwaukee is the second-highest city in America per capita for bars. There's one bar per 1,800 people here.

But of all of the bars, here are some of the most popular: the Lost Whale, HiHat Lounge, Blu, The Sofie, Belmont Tavern, The Jazz Estate, Wolski's Tavern, Tied House Milwaukee, Newsroom Pub, Nomad World Pub, Jack's American Pub, Duke's on Water, The Wicked Hop, WürstBar, Thurmans 15, Red Lion British Pub, Y-Not II Tavern, Nashville North, Pete's Pub, The Pharmacy Bar, Finks, Jamo's, The Garage, Malone's on Brady, Jo-Cats Pub, Angelo's Piano Lounge, Up-Down MKE, Club

Brady, First and Bowl, Central Standard Crafthouse & Kitchen Bar, The Mothership, Vendetta Coffee Bar, Aperitivo, Riley's Social House, The Drunken Cobra, 3rd Street Market Hall, Tropic MKE, Daq Shack, Shaker's Cigar Bar, The Bar at Saint Kate, and The Explorium Brewpub Third Ward—just to name a few!

Figure 20 An example of popular signage around bars in Milwaukee.

RENOWNED RESTAURANTS

There are several restaurants around town that have been compared to those that are Michelin starred. They include the following:

Odd Duck
$$$

939 S. 2nd Street
Milwaukee, WI 53204

Phone: (414) 763-5881
Oddduckrestaurant.com

Hours of Operation
Tuesday – Saturday
Bar: 3 p.m. to 12 a.m.
Kitchen: 5 p.m. to 10 p.m.

This small-plate restaurant features creative cocktails and a shared-plate menu that is constantly changing. Odd Duck has an upbeat atmosphere.

Sanford Restaurant
$$$$

1547 N. Jackson Street
Milwaukee, WI 53202

Phone: (414) 276-9608
Sanfordrestaurant.com

Hours of Operation
Tuesday – Friday: 5:30 to 9 p.m.
Saturday: 5 to 10 p.m.

Sanford Restaurant is an elegant venue that offers creative and upscale New American fare and wine.

Ardent
$$$$

1751 N. Farwell Avenue
Milwaukee, WI 53202

Phone: (414) 897-7022
Ardentmke.com

Hours of Operation
Wednesday – Saturday: 5 to 11 p.m.

Ardent Restaurant is an intimate, upscale choice that presents innovative New American fare, including a tasting menu.

The Chef's Table

500 S. 3rd Street
Milwaukee, WI 53204

Phone: (414) 277-7676
Chefs-tablemke.com
info@chefstablemke.com

This is the only personalized private event venue and dining experience in Milwaukee. You can reserve rooms for small gatherings, weddings, corporate events, etc., and each will come with a unique menu.

Bacchus – A Bartolotta Restaurant
$$$$

925 E. Wells Street
Milwaukee, WI 53202

Phone: (414) 765-1166
Bartolottas.com

Hours of operation
Wednesday – Saturday: 5 to 9 p.m.

Bacchus is a sleek, upscale New American spot with an extensive wine list and a conservatory overlooking Lake Michigan.

Bartolotta's Lake Park Bistro
$$$$

3133 E. Newberry Boulevard
Milwaukee, WI 53211

Phone: (414) 962-6300
Bartolottas.com

Hours of operation
Monday – Saturday: 5 to 9 p.m.

This quaint bistro features upscale French fare, an extensive wine list, and views of Lake Michigan.

La Merenda
$$

125 E. National Avenue
Milwaukee, WI 53204

Phone: (414) 389-0125
Lamerenda125.com

Hours of operation
Monday – Thursday: 11 a.m. to 2 p.m., 5 to 9 p.m.
Friday: 11 a.m. to 2 p.m., 5 to 10 p.m.
Saturday: 5 to 10 p.m.

La Merenda means "early snack" in Italian, and this tapas restaurant is known for being a colorful spot with an outdoor bar and a global menu of small plates, beers, and wine.

Harbor House
$$$

550 N. Harbor Drive
Milwaukee, WI 53202

Phone: (414) 395-4900
Bartolottas.com

Hours of operation
Monday, Wednesday – Friday: 5 to 9 p.m.
Saturday: 11 a.m. to 2 p.m., 5 to 9 p.m.
Sunday: 11 a.m. to 2 p.m., 5 to 9 p.m.

Harbor House is considered an upscale restaurant that offers skyline and Lake Michigan views. Steak, seafood dishes, and a great wine list are offered and served.

Black Sheep
$$

216 S. 2nd Street
Milwaukee, WI 53204

Phone: (414) 223-0903
Blacksheepmke.com

Hours of operation
Monday – Thursday: 11 a.m. to 10 p.m.
Friday: 11 a.m. to 12 a.m.
Saturday: 10 a.m. to 12 a.m.

Sunday: 10 a.m. to 4 p.m.

Black Sheep is a hip spot with craft wines on tap, cocktails, and elevated bar fare. It has a sleek and modern interior.

The Noble
$$

704 S. 2nd Street
Milwaukee, WI 53204

Phone: (414) 243-4997
Nobleprovisions.com

Hours of operation
Monday: 11 a.m. to 3 p.m.
Thursday – Saturday: 5 to 9 p.m.

This restaurant serves brunch, cocktails, and New American fare. The Noble offers a warm space and outdoor seating.

Rare Steakhouse
$$$$

833 E. Michigan Street
Milwaukee, WI 53202

Phone: (414) 273-7273
Raresteaks.com

Hours of operation
Monday – Thursday: 4 to 9 p.m.
Friday – Saturday: 4 to 10 p.m.

As the name suggests, Rare Steakhouse is an upscale steakhouse that boasts a traditional vibe. Classy cuts of meat, rich sides, and perfectly paired fine wines are served here.

Three Brothers
$$

2412 S. St. Clair Street
Milwaukee, WI 53207

Phone: (414) 481-7530
Threebrothersmke.com

Hours of operation
Wednesday – Friday: 5 to 9 p.m.
Saturday – Sunday: 4 to 9 p.m.

This Serbian restaurant has been a favorite spot for Milwaukeeans for three generations. It is considered "low-key" and has a vintage storefront setting.

Red Light Ramen
$$
1749 N. Farwell Avenue
Milwaukee, WI 53202

Phone: (414) 837-5107
Redlightramen.com

Hours of operation
Sunday – Saturday: 5 to 10 p.m.

Red Light Ramen is an intimate setting that, of course, serves ramen. Dishes are paired with sides, sake, beer, wine, and boozy slushies.

Centraal Grand Café & Tappery
$$

2306 S. Kinnickinnic Avenue
Milwaukee, Wisconsin 53207

Phone: (414) 755-0378
Cafecentraal.com

Hours of operation
Monday – Thursday: 8 a.m. to 10 p.m.
Friday – Saturday: 8 a.m. to 11 p.m.
Sunday: 8 a.m. to 9 p.m.

This European-style café features a vast menu of Belgian and Dutch beers and food. There is also outdoor seating available.

The Diplomat
$$

815 E. Brady Street
Milwaukee, WI 53202
Phone: (414) 800-5816
Thediplomatmke.com

Hours of operation
Wednesday – Saturday: 4 to 9 p.m.

The Diplomat serves American classics with a contemporary edge and inventive cocktails.

Stella Van Buren
$$$

550 N. Van Buren Street
Milwaukee, WI 53202

Phone: (414) 847-5622
Stellavanburen.com

Hours of operation
Monday – Friday: 6:30 a.m. to 10 p.m.
Saturday – Sunday: 7 to 11 a.m., 5 to 10 p.m.

COFFEE SHOPS

Figure 21 Colectivo Coffee was founded 30 years ago in Milwaukee.

Milwaukeeans also take coffee pretty seriously. The best coffee shops include Rochambo Coffee & Tea House, Interval, Alderaan Coffee, Colectivo Coffee, Dryhootch Coffeehouse, Likewise Coffee, Fairgrounds Coffee and Tea, Pilcrow Coffee, Nomad Coffee Bar, Anodyne Coffee Roasting Co., Stone Creek Coffee, Roast Coffee Company, Coffee Makes You Black, Discourse Coffee, Grace Place Coffee, and Canary Coffee Bar.

STREET FOOD

Figure 22 A taco vendor located in the Walker's Point neighborhood.

There are also several street vendors that provide delicious food. Pig Tailz MKE, Get Them While They're Hot Tamales, Real Dogs, Ofelia's Food Truck, George's Big Dogs, Tudo Sabor Brasil, Freddy's Tacos, Velspresso, Taco Moto, The Good Food Dude, SE Azn Cuizine on Wheelz, Red Truck Sliders, Freddy's, JC King's Tortas, Kealohas, Buddha's BBQ, Pedro's South American Food, Lumpia City, Pina Mexican Eats, Press, Smoked at 225, and Happy Dough Lucky are just some of them. (A full list of all of the food trucks around Milwaukee can be found on visitmilwaukee.org.)

SHOPPING

Markets & Shops

Milwaukee Public Market

Figure 23 The Milwaukee Public Market is located in the Historic Third Ward neighborhood.

"A gathering place where great taste is always in season."

In Milwaukee's Historic Third Ward is the "industrial chic" Marketplace that offers local baked goods, meats, produce, alcoholic drinks, coffee, sushi, and prepared eats.

After it opened in 2005, Milwaukee historian, John Gurda, said, "The facility is rooted in an old tradition. Long after the novelty wears off, the Public Market will remain the freshest landmark in downtown Milwaukee."

Figure 24 Inside the Milwaukee Public Market

There are also cooking classes, weddings, and other events that occur on a regular basis in the market.

More information can be found at milwaukeepublicmarket.org.

<u>Glorioso's Italian Market</u>

Open on Milwaukee's East Side for over 70 years, the 10,000-square-foot Glorioso's

Italian Market is a deli and store filled with Mediterranean-Italian foods. Perusing the aisles and grabbing a snack at this market is truly a unique experience. And if you spend enough time there, you might forget that you aren't actually in Italy!

Usinger's Famous Sausage

This historic deli is on the riverfront in Milwaukee, and it includes a deli with extensive meats available to order, along with a gift shop that offers meat (70 different varieties), cheese, and other items to be used in spreads for special occasions or alongside everyday dinners!

Antiques on Pierce

This 50,000 square foot, three-floored antique store was opened in June 2015, and it is the largest mall of its kind in southeastern Wisconsin. It showcases items, including vintage clothing, jewelry, furniture, glassware, toys, etc., from over 100 dealers.

Bayshore

Bayshore, located in the neighboring town of Glendale, is an open-air shopping mall/mixed-use complex including retail shops, restaurants, offices, and apartments. There's also a large grassy section called "The Yard," with a large television that shows local sports games and movies for locals to gather and enjoy together.

Souvenirs to Bring Home

Of course, the first thought when bringing a souvenir home from Wisconsin is either beer or cheese. But other items, such as collectible mugs, clothing, or other items available throughout Milwaukee, make great souvenirs. It really depends on what you do when you get here, but it's safe to say that you'll find a keepsake to remind you of your trip for years to come!

Fun fact: did you know that the foam "Cheesehead" hat most commonly associated with Green Bay Packers fans was made in Milwaukee? It's true; it was—by a company called Foamation Inc.

ENTERTAINMENT

Figure 25 Pabst Theatre in Downtown Milwaukee.

There are venues—large and small—designed for live music throughout the city.

MUSIC/ENTERTAINMENT VENUES

The Pabst Theater Group

Website: pabsttheatergroup.com

1) <u>The Pabst Theater</u>

144 E. Wells Street
Milwaukee, WI 53202

Opened: November 9, 1895
Capacity: 1,279

This theater was designed to resemble a European opera house, it's able to accommodate just about any performing art form, and it is located in Milwaukee's downtown theater district. It hosts about 100 events every year. Tip: Anytime I've ever been to this space, the box office has been hard to locate—it's also been confusing as to where to enter the building. I'd recommend arriving early.

Upcoming events: Postmodern Jukebox, Sparks, Jinkx Monsoon, The Sinatra Experience, Fresh Coast Jazz Festival, Stephen Sanchez, and the Wailin' Jennys.

2) The Riverside Theater

116 W. Wisconsin Avenue
Milwaukee, WI 53203

Opened: 1928
Capacity: 2,450

Named for its location along the Milwaukee River,
this is one of Milwaukee's opulent theaters that
welcomes the highest caliber of artists. Tip: One
event (Schitt's Creek: Up Close and Personal) I
attended had poor security management, and
everyone had to form an incredibly long and slow-
moving line outside. So, again, I'd recommend
arriving early.

Upcoming Events: Taylor Tomlinson, Death Cab for
Cutie, Kansas, RuPaul's Drag Race Live, Ben Folds,
The Piano Guys, Bonnie Raitt, and The Irish Tenors.

3) Turner Hall Ballroom

1040 N. Vel R. Phillips Avenue
Milwaukee, WI 53203

Opened: 1883
Capacity: 300 for dinner, 250 for dinner and dancing,
and 500 for a standing reception.

This ballroom is located in Turner Hall, a National Historic Landmark. It is the perfect place for eclectic shows for all ages and cultures.

Upcoming events: David Cross, Martin Sexton & KT Tunstall, Pete Holmes, Hunter Hayes, and Rory Scovel.

4) The Back Room @ Colectivo

> 2211 N. Prospect Avenue
> Milwaukee, WI 53202

Located in the back (hence the name) of the Colectivo coffee shop on Prospect Avenue, this is a great place to get up close and personal with the next upcoming artists.

Upcoming events: Willie Watson, Pedro the Lion, The Samples, Michigander, John R. Miller, and Daniel Villarreal.

5) Miller High Life Theatre

> Opened: 1909

500 W. Kilbourn Avenue
Milwaukee, WI 53203

A 4,087-seat venue with two sloped tiers of seats that provide a great view and comfort.

Upcoming Events: An Evening with Alice Cooper, Paw Patrol Live!, Dino Ranch Live, Los Tigres Del Norte, and Time Allen.

The Rave/Eagles Club/The Eagles Ballroom

2401 W. Wisconsin Avenue
Milwaukee, WI 53233

Opened: 1926
Capacity: 400 to 4,000

Website: therave.com

This music venue hosts national and local artists in a historic 1920s building with six performance spaces. Tip: the surrounding areas are not known to be the safest. Take necessary precautions.

Upcoming events: Julieta Venegas, All Time Low, Nekrogoblikon, grandson / k.flay, Prof, The Dead South, and Macklemore.

Warner Grand Theater (also known as the Bradley Symphony Center)

212 W. Wisconsin Avenue
Milwaukee, WI 53203
Opened: May 1, 1931

This Art Deco-inspired location is currently under reconstruction, but it will be the house for the Milwaukee Symphony Orchestra.

Figure 26 The new electronic blade sign for Warner Theater.

Marcus Performance Arts Center

929 N. Water Street
Milwaukee, WI 53202

Opened: July 26, 1969
Capacity: 2,125

Website: marcuscenter.org

The Marcus Center is the premier presenter of performing arts, including Broadway shows. It is also the home to the Milwaukee Ballet. Shows for the 2022/2023 season include Frozen: The Hit Broadway Musical, Six: The Musical, My Fair Lady, Tootsie: The Comedy Musical, Hairspray, Hadestown, and Les Miserables.

Skylight Music Theatre

Opened: 1959
Capacity: 358

Website: skylightmusictheatre.org

158 N. Broadway
Milwaukee, WI 53202

This vintage venue gives over 90 performances each season, mainly focusing on emerging American talent.

Upcoming events: SuperYou and The Song of Bernadette: A New Musical.

Other Venues

There are several other entertainment centers throughout the city, including the Milwaukee Repertory Theater, The Boulevard Theatre, The Alchemist Theatre, The Northern Lights Theater, the Milwaukee Theatre, Milwaukee Chamber Theatre,

Brumder Mansion Theater, Quadracci Powerhouse Theater, the Milwaukee Entertainment Group, and the Miramir Theatre.

FESTIVALS

Figure 6 Milwaukee's Summerfest (the world's largest music festival) draws hundreds of thousands of people into the heart of the city every summer.

Also known as the "city of Festivals," Milwaukee has a TON of festivals throughout the year. There are musical festivals, cultural festivals, food festivals, seasonal festivals, and more. Here is a breakdown of the festivals that occur in and around Milwaukee based on the four seasons.

March

- International Anime Music Festival
- Shamrock Shuffle
- MobCraft's Sour Fest
- Milwaukee Public Museum's Food & Froth
- Milwaukee Blues Festival

April

- Milwaukee Film Festival

May

- Lager and Friends Beer Festival

June

- Pridefest
- Crusher Fest
- Milwaukee Highland Games
- West Allis A La Carte
- Polishfest
- Milwaukee Water Lantern Festival
- Brewtown Rumble
- Lakefront Festival of Art
- Summer Soulstice
- Juneteenth Celebration
- Summerfest Weekend 1 & 2*
- Cedarburg Strawberry Festival
- Family 4th Fest*

- Franklin Civic Celebration*

  *- These events tend to lead into July.

July

- Glendale 4th of July Celebration
- Whitefish Bay 4th of July
- Summerfest Weekend 3
- Whitefish Bay Art Fest
- Homegrown Music Festival
- Midsummer Festival of Arts
- Croatian Fest
- Armenian Fest
- Germanfest
- Milwaukee Brewfest
- Bastille Days

August

- Black Arts Fest MKE
- Jewish Food Festival
- Greendale Village Days
- Irish Fest
- Art & Chalk Fest
- Brew City Cigar Festival
- West Bend GERMANfest
- Country in the Burg
- Fresh Coast Jazz Festival
- Octoberfest
- Mexican Fiesta

- Brady Street Festival
- Bloody Mary Festival
- Taco Fest (although sometimes in September)

September

- Saint Francis Days
- Third Ward Art Festival
- Laborfest
- Tosa Fest
- Trimborn Farm Arts and Harvest
- Cedarburg Wine & Harvest Festival
- Fromm Petfest

Fall (Only October has festivals)

October

- Greenfield Fall Family Fest
- Cedarburg Octoberfest
- West Bend Fall Fest

January

- Gift of Wings Cool Fool Kite Festival
- N/A Day: "Dry January" Beverage Festival
- Ice Bear Fest
- Winterfest at Boerner Botanical Gardens

February

- Burnhearts Mitten Fest
- Sweets and Treats Fest
- Cedarburg Winter Festival
- Mama Tried Motorcycle Show
- Jazz Heritage Festival

Milwaukee might not be the No. 1 place people think to visit when planning a trip, but I hope this guide has proved that it's actually the perfect place for a vacation! First of all, especially during the summer months, there are endless things to do—from attending one of the festivals, hiking through nature, strolling a RiverWalk, exploring a museum, touring a brewery, hanging out on the water, shopping at our unique markets and malls, or going to a live concert or performance. I promise, no matter your interests, you'll find the perfect activities for you. Plus, you're sure to be surrounded by hospitable and kind Midwesterners the whole time you're here. If you want to feel like a local, you can simply just call a water fountain a "bubbler," say, "Er no?" after asking any question—even if you're sure of the answer, or act unsurprised when your bloody mary comes with a beer chaser.

For more information about Milwaukee, you can visit the follow websites:
Milwaukee365.com

READ OTHER TRAVEL BOOKS FROM CZYK PUBLISHING

Greater Than a Tourist- California: 50 Travel Tips from Locals

Greater Than a Tourist- Salem Massachusetts USA 50 Travel Tips from a Local by Danielle Lasher

Greater Than a Tourist United States: 50 Travel Tips from Locals

Greater Than a Tourist- St. Croix US Virgin Islands USA: 50 Travel Tips from a Local by Tracy Birdsall

Greater Than a Tourist- Montana: 50 Travel Tips from a Local by Laurie White

Children's Book: Charlie the Cavalier Travels the World by Lisa Rusczyk Ed. D.

CZYKPublishing.com

METRIC CONVERSIONS

TEMPERATURE

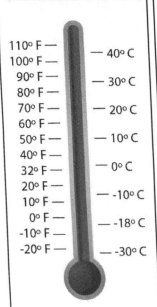

110° F —	— 40° C
100° F —	
90° F —	— 30° C
80° F —	
70° F —	— 20° C
60° F —	
50° F —	— 10° C
40° F —	
32° F —	— 0° C
20° F —	
10° F —	— -10° C
0° F —	
-10° F —	— -18° C
-20° F —	— -30° C

To convert F to C:

Subtract 32, and then multiply by 5/9 or .5555.

To Convert C to F:

Multiply by 1.8 and then add 32.

32F = 0C

LIQUID VOLUME

To Convert:.................Multiply by	
U.S. Gallons to Liters................	3.8
U.S. Liters to Gallons	26
Imperial Gallons to U.S. Gallons	1.2
Imperial Gallons to Liters......	4.55
Liters to Imperial Gallons	22

1 Liter = .26 U.S. Gallon
1 U.S. Gallon = 3.8 Liters

DISTANCE

To convert ....Multiply by	
Inches to Centimeters 2.54	
Centimeters to Inches 39	
Feet to Meters......................	.3
Meters to Feet	3.28
Yards to Meters	91
Meters to Yards	1.09
Miles to Kilometers	1.61
Kilometers to Miles............	.62

1 Mile = 1.6 km
1 km = .62 Miles

WEIGHT

1 Ounce = .28 Grams
1 Pound = .4555 Kilograms
1 Gram = .04 Ounce
1 Kilogram = 2.2 Pounds

Printed in Great Britain
by Amazon